A TAX ON ALL THE PEOPLE

THE POLL TAX

CAREY OPPENHEIM

Research and Information Officer, CPAG

D0726763

CPAG Ltd
1-5 Bath Street, London EC1V 9PY
December 1987

© CPAG Limited 1987
ISBN 0 946744 06 8

The views expressed in this publication are not necessarily those of the Child Poverty Action Group

Cover design and Peasants' Revolt drawing by Clifford Harper
Typeset by Nancy White
Printed by Calvert's North Star Press, 31-39 Redchurch Street, London E2

Contents

Acknowledgements

Many thanks to my many readers — Fran Bennett, Geoff Fimister, Peter Golding, Professor John Stewart, Tony Travers and Paul Wilding — for their very valuable comments. Special thanks to Peter Ridpath, Nancy White and Calverts at a time when we are without a publications production worker.

Foreword

'And it came to pass in those days that there went out a decree . . . that all the world should be taxed.' (The Gospel According to St Luke, chapter 2, verse 1, Authorised Version of The Holy Bible)

The Conservative Party has for some time maintained that it wished to abolish the system of domestic rates, and its election manifesto in 1987 contained the promise that rates for households would be replaced by a 'community charge' on individuals. Despite valiant efforts by the government to impress the term 'community charge' upon the public consciousness, however, the proposed new levy has generally become known as the 'poll tax'; indeed, the Prime Minister on one occasion inadvertently used the phrase herself. We therefore refer to the community charge as the 'poll tax' throughout this pamphlet.

The proposals to introduce a poll tax are of concern to CPAG for three main reasons. First, they are unfair. Despite the government's pre-election pledge to compensate the poorest for their minimum contribution (probably 20%) to the poll tax, it appears that many low income families in high-rated areas will lose out, because the compensation is likely to be calculated as an average across the whole country. Even leaving aside the probability that many people will not take up those means-tested benefits which entitle them to the rebate, this must be of concern to CPAG, especially since families with children are generally acknowledged to face some of the most difficult problems in trying to exist on already inadequate benefit levels. Such families may also face resentment from others on low incomes, but above the qualifying level for rebates, who have to pay the full charge.

This is the basis for the second reason for CPAG's concern about the poll tax: that it is unjust. Whilst our primary focus must be the impact of the poll tax on poor families, we cannot but be disturbed at a system of taxation which — above a certain level of income — takes no account of differential ability to pay (or of what is often known as 'taxable capacity'). Principles of redistributive justice and fairness are not limited, in our view, to those below a particular (often narrowly defined) 'poverty line', but should be applied across the income scale in both national and local taxation systems. This principle of progressivity has long been accepted in all political parties as the basis of the taxation of personal incomes at a national level; the current system of domestic rates reflects this principle (though imperfectly — see Chapter 2), since the rateable value of properties tends to reflect the income and/or wealth of their occupants. But the government's poll tax proposals abandon the principle entirely.

Thirdly, we believe that the poll tax proposals are undemocratic. CPAG has for many years been concerned not only about the incomes of the poor but also about their ability to participate fully in society. Fundamental to such a concern is the ability of the poor to participate in the institutions of democracy and to benefit from the provision of services (see *Excluding the Poor*, ed Peter Golding, CPAG, 1986). There is widespread anxiety that the compilation of registers to ensure that everyone pays the poll tax will include a scrutiny of both the electoral register and any available list of users of local services (such as libraries, swimming pools and day centres). These local services are used in particular, of course, by families with dependent children. A tax which creates an incentive, especially for those on lower incomes, to disenfranchise themselves and to opt out of using facilities available to the general population appears to us to be seriously flawed.

Several other attempts to institute a poll tax in this country — in 1377, 1379 and 1381 — ended in tears, with the Peasants' Revolt of 1381. The historian, T F Tout, concluded that 'The fault was a mulish determination to enforce a thoroughly distasteful order in the face of public opposition' (quoted in the *Financial Times*, 5 September 1987). There is considerable — and growing — public opposition to the proposals for the introduction of another version of the poll tax, over six hundred years later. Whilst the legislation to introduce the poll tax in Scotland in 1989 is already on the statute book, at the time of writing the Bill to introduce it in England and Wales (from 1990 to 1994) has not yet been published. We hope that this pamphlet will contribute to the body of information available about the 'community charge' and its likely effects, and that the concerns expressed above, which are shared by a wide range of people across the political spectrum, will be communicated to those in a position to influence the proposals as they are debated both in Parliament and by a wider public.

Fran Bennett
Director, CPAG   November 1987

Introduction

'The poll tax is fair only in the sense that the Black Death was fair; it is indiscriminate, striking at young and old, rich and poor, employed and unemployed alike.'

(Tory Reform Group, 1987)

Imagine a system of local taxation which halves the tax burden of the richest, shifts resources from the recession-struck North to the affluent South East, boosts already soaring house prices, costs at least twice as much to collect as the system it is designed to replace, necessitates an army of investigators to trace those liable to pay it, disenfranchises the poorest, and introduces a system of rebates so complicated that few can understand it. This is what the Community Charge will bring.

The Community Charge is known as the 'poll tax' because it is a flat-rate payment per adult citizen. Bearing equally heavily on the lowest paid hospital cleaner as on the highest paid city executive, it has aroused widespread hostility and anger. Taxation is, after all, the underside of the welfare state. Local taxation, like national taxation, should take account of people's ability to pay — or so it has been assumed almost universally in the past.

The government's general tax strategy has produced a marked shift in the tax burden *from* the rich *to* the poor, brought about by the reduction in the top rate of tax, the drop in the basic rate of tax (the least effective way of targeting tax cuts on those who need them most)[1] and the rise in indirect taxes. The Community Charge is the latest addition to a highly regressive package.

This pamphlet is a brief guide to the proposals. It is not a technical analysis, but an attempt to highlight the central issues. It does not deal in detail with the proposals for the business rate and the central grant system except in so far as they interact with the Community Charge. Chapter 1 paints in the background to the changes, placing the Community Charge in the context of central government policy towards local government. Chapter 2 goes on to deal with the arguments and counter-arguments for abolishing rates. This is followed in Chapter 3 with a simple guide to the

1

Community Charge — what it is and how it will work. Chapter 4 addresses the case for and against the Community Charge, looking at technical adequacy, fairness, local accountability and the impact on social security claimants. Chapter 5 examines the effects of the changes by income and family type, and on regions, ethnic minorities and local authorities. Finally, there is a brief look at other options for reform.

The analysis shows that the contradiction between the government's rhetoric of concern for the poorest, the regions with high rates of unemployment and the inner cities, and the actual effects of the introduction of the Community Charge, could not be starker. For the Community Charge will fall most heavily on the poorest citizens in the North and in the inner cities. As the Child Poverty Action Group said in its response to the Green Paper *Paying for Local Government:* 'In the context of the latest official figures of nearly 16.4m people living in or on the margins of poverty, CPAG is especially anxious that the Government is proposing a system of local government finance which will fall most heavily on the poorest sections of society.'[2]

References
1 See R Lister, *Building One Nation*, CPAG, 1987.
2 *A Feudal Levy*, CPAG, 1986.

Chapter 1

Setting the scene

Introduction

The Conservative government's long-standing promise to abolish rates had widely been assumed to be empty. But in 1986 its glossy Green Paper, *Paying for Local Government*, once again made rates a live political issue, with its proposal for a Community Charge, which has since then generally come to be called the 'poll tax'.

The poll tax is already a reality for Scotland. The Abolition of Domestic Rates (Scotland) Act is now in force. Scotland has the unenviable pleasure of being the testing ground for the poll tax in 1989. Wales and England will follow in 1990. However, in 13 London local authorities, where the poll tax would be particularly high, it will be phased in over a four-year period, to be fully operational in 1994.

The reforms involve the radical overhaul of local authority finance as we know it. A flat rate poll tax, levied locally on all adults aged 18 or over (with a few exemptions), will replace domestic rates; a uniform business rate will be set; and the allocation of central government grant to local authorities will be changed.

The poll tax can *only* be understood in the context of the Conservative government's approach to local government since 1979 — hence the need to set the scene in some detail.

The central theme behind the reforms is the superficially attractive one of 'local accountability'. The government defines this as making explicit the links between voting, paying for and using local authority services. 'Effective local accountability must be the cornerstone of successful local government. All too often this accountability is blurred and weakened by the complexities of the national grant system and by the fact that differences arise among those who vote for, those who pay for and those who receive local government services.'[1] But how real is this 'local accountability'?

3

Centralisation

The last two Conservative governments can boast a legacy of major changes in central government financial support for local government: 10 or 11 different systems have operated since 1979; the Greater London Council and the metropolitan counties have been abolished;[2] and central government grants to local authorities have been reduced from about two thirds of net local authority spending to just under half. The poll tax is part and parcel of the government's strategy for both expenditure control and political control of local authorities.

The programme of the government following the 1987 election has again put local government at the top of the political agenda. Schools are to be encouraged to opt out of local education authority control. Within the Inner London Education Authority (ILEA) whole boroughs can opt out and it seems likely that Westminster, Kensington and Chelsea, and Wandsworth will do so. Council tenants are to be encouraged to swap their local authority landlords for housing associations or co-operatives. Housing Action Trusts are to be formed from the private sector with the power to take over and renovate parts of, or whole, housing estates. Both moves are attempts to end the local authority monopoly of two of their largest services — education and housing.

The Local Government Bill will restrict local authority power in a number of ways. Local authorities will be forced to put out to competitive tendering refuse collection, cleaning, catering (including school meals and meals on wheels), and garden and vehicle maintenance services. They will no longer have the power to impose 'contract compliance' (ie, conditions on private contractors to ensure adequate minimum wages and working conditions, adequate health and safety, and non-discrimination on the grounds of sex, race or disability, or to safeguard employment opportunities for people from the local area). All local authority publicity on 'political' or 'controversial' areas will be severely curtailed.[3]

But it is the much publicised 'inner city' policy which highlights the government's attitude to local authorities. The inner city package includes the extension of Urban Development Corporations. (These are independent, non-elected bodies funded mostly by central government, with the aim of attracting private companies to develop run-down areas without the restriction of planning controls. Too often, little attention is paid to the needs of the local communities concerned. The best known example is the London Docklands.) Inner City Task Forces, City Technology Colleges and special training opportunities are some of the other elements of the package. While it might be argued that private sector funds could be a welcome addition to inner city areas, the proposals are clearly aimed at by-passing local authority control.[4]

Murray Stewart, Director of the School for Advanced Urban Studies, has criticised this approach to the problems of inner cities: 'Ministers' analysis is that the inner city is an area of physical decay marked by a kind of fecklessness of the local population, induced by incompetent local authorities. Yet apart from perhaps small pockets, there is little evidence that this is true, nor does it help in forming a coherent strategy.'[5]

The Audit Commission has estimated that, if all the government proposals on local authorities are implemented, local authority spending could decline by as much as 30% from £30bn to £20.9bn over five years, with a drop of 37% in manpower (though some of this will transfer to the private sector).[6] 'Plans for the destruction of local democracy are now complete. The government's tanks are moving into place around every town hall. Battle will commence in the autumn. From then on local government is likely to suffer a series of blows from which it will be extremely fortunate to recover. Britain will be more than ever a centrally managed state, with power concentrated in Whitehall.'[7]

This centralisation will remove decision-making from local authorities to central government ministers and bureaucrats. Contrary to the rhetoric of 'local accountability', it will further remove power from electors.

The poll tax fits neatly into this framework. As is shown later, the changes to local government finance will *decrease* local authority control over local spending; increases in spending will be at the expense of local residents (see pp 16-17); and local authorities will be encouraged to widen the scope of the services for which they charge.

The rationale for reform

The speech which Nicholas Ridley (Secretary of State for the Environment) gave in Liverpool on 3 August 1987 is the clearest exposition of the government's rationale for reform in local government finance. It is useful to look more closely at that rationale.

High spending
First, the government believes that local authorities' (and the nation's) problems begin from high spending. That is the starting point in the causal chain:

> The Labour Party in local government, especially the extremists, always over-bid others in their promises to spend, spend, spend,

5

because it alone is prepared to sacrifice the interests of the local economy and drive away jobs in private firms by ill-concealed bribes in the form of higher spending and higher subsidies for those who do not have to pay the bills... This cycle of decline: high spending leading to high rates, leading to job losses, leading to poverty and higher needs and higher spending and higher rates, can only be broken when those who vote in local elections are aware of the costs of local authority services as well as the benefits.

So, in the view of the government, it is the Labour local authorities themselves which are to blame for their problems. Spending is not directed to services genuinely needed by the local populace but is to be regarded as 'bribes' to a self-interested electorate.

There is, of course, an alternative explanation: that social and economic needs — high unemployment, high dependency on supplementary benefit, inner city degeneration — are the starting point. Spending is the proper and considered response to appalling social and economic problems. The Audit Commission[8] highlighted management problems in *London* inner city local authorities, but also pinpointed some of the particular problems of these areas — male unemployment rates of 45%, poor housing, growing homelessness, 50% more crime in London's metropolitan areas than outside, and lone parents making up four out of 10 families. The alternative analysis of local authority difficulties starts from the needs which are the result of changing economic and social conditions in those inner city heartlands.

Political control
The second link in the chain is political. As Nicholas Ridley said: 'Above all, the new system will remove from Liverpool that poisonous power base on which extremism thrives — the power base of spending power without local accountability.'

The government is concerned both about Labour control of local councils and about Labour MPs' continued dominance in inner cities. As a writer for the *Sunday Times* put it: 'In Liverpool, Manchester, Glasgow and Newcastle where much of the worst inner-city conditions are found, there is now not a single Conservative Member of Parliament. Labour domination, at least in the town hall and council chambers, is almost as complete... Ridley with the lion's share of the inner-city budget takes the hardest line over freezing out the uncooperative authorities.'[9]

But, as the *Financial Times* leader says: 'There are many reasons why a healthy local democracy ought to be nurtured. It is not necessarily a bad thing that opposition parties should be able to capture local centres of power, partly as a training ground for national office, and partly as a means of enabling local communities to vote the other way if they so choose. Local institutions are by definition more likely to be aware of local needs than are far-off officials.'[10]

Dependency

The third link in the chain of government argument is ideological. A recurrent theme is the dislike of the damaging dependency which is supposed to be the product of high levels of spending and service provision. Labour local authorities are charged with fostering such dependency on welfare, which the government sees as anathema to its ethic of enterprise culture and self-reliance. Nicholas Ridley said: 'They [local authorities] can reinforce the climate of dependency in which people — wrongly but understandably — see state provision and state spending as their way of life. As more people become dependent on the council, so the extremists' power grows.'

This foreshadows the speech made by John Moore, the Secretary of State for Social Services, on 26 September 1987, in which he contrasts the 'sullen apathy of dependence' with the 'sheer delight of personal achievement'. He urges that the spirit of self-help and enterprise be extended to the welfare state. Most importantly, he sees the welfare state as fostering dependence. According to his view, the welfare state itself causes the very poverty it aims to relieve.

This interpretation of dependence is based on a false belief that people can be entirely independent from one another. In fact, everyone is dependent in different ways and at different times. It assumes that people voluntarily choose to be dependent on the state, local or national, rather than being forced into dependency by poverty and unemployment over which they have no control. What is wrong in being 'dependent' on having someone collect your dustbin refuse, or provide street lighting or parks?

A charge for services

The final link in Nicholas Ridley's speech is the equation of local authority services with consumer goods in the market place. The poll tax, instead of being a tax related to people's ability to pay, should be seen as a charge for services, like the price of tomatoes in a shop. Actually, the closest analogy is a television licence fee — a flat-rate charge which is not related to level of income or consumption. Everybody pays the same and then uses the facility in their own way.

'The Community Charge', he argues, 'will be a flat rate charge for local services. It has to be a flat rate charge because crucial to

7

the change is the concept that there should be a "price" for local government services. Like prices for goods in the shops, the Community Charge "price" can only work properly if it is roughly the same for everyone.'[11]

But local authority services are not properly to be regarded as commodities bought and sold in the market. As Professor Jones and A Travers write: 'Local authorities are elected bodies set up to fulfil political objectives, one of the most important of which is to decide on the balance between public and private provision... Local government is not just to deliver a set service for a set sum, but to govern in the light of community preferences, which include decisions on redistributive issues.'[12]

Opposition

There has been widespread opposition to the proposals from public bodies such as the Rating and Valuation Association, the Confederation of British Industry, the National Campaign for Civil Liberties and many more, from the wider public and from within Conservative ranks. The response to the consultation exercise on the Green Paper showed that 283 submissions were in favour of a poll tax and 565 were against it.[13]

A Gallup poll carried out for the *Daily Telegraph* (27 July 1987) showed that:

- 54% thought that the poll tax was a bad idea
- 28% thought that the poll tax was a good idea
- 18% did not know

- 47% of people thought that the proposed system would not be as fair as the current system
- 27% of people thought that the proposed system would be fairer
- 6% of people thought that there was no difference
- 19% of people did not know

Among Conservatives, although 46% thought that the proposals were a good idea, 36% thought they were a bad idea. The latest MORI poll (*Sunday Times*, 4 October 1987) confirms that a growing majority oppose the changes; it showed that 58% thought the poll tax a bad thing, while only 30% approved; 67% thought that the better off should pay more, while 25% thought they should pay the same.

The government is determined to see through the changes, despite the consistent opposition both of a majority of the general public and of a substantial number of Conservative politicians.

Summary

'Local accountability' is the government's justification for the poll tax. But, as the chapter shows, changes since 1979 have centralised local government's finances and weakened its political voice. The planned reforms, ranging from education, housing, inner cities, and the Local Government Bill, to the poll tax, will continue the process of curtailing local authority power. In the government's view, the vicious circle of high spending and high rates, which it identifies as the principal problem, can only be broken by making the local electorate bear the consequences of voting for high spending. The chosen mechanism is the poll tax. Despite widespread opposition, the government is sticking to its task.

References

1 Foreword to the Green Paper, *Paying for Local Government*, Cmnd 9714.
2 G Jones and J Stewart, *The Guardian*, 23 April 1986.
3 See *Low Pay Review* 29, Spring 1987.
4 See Employment Institute, *Inner City Initiatives*, 1987.
5 *The Independent*, 18 August 1987.
6 *Financial Times*, 13 July 1987.
7 *Financial Times*, 17 August 1987.
8 *The Management of London's Local Authorities*, January 1987.
9 *Sunday Times*, 21 June 1987.
10 *Financial Times*, 30 June 1987.
11 Extract from speech by Rt Hon Nicholas Ridley MP, Secretary of State for the Environment, Liverpool, 3 August 1987.
12 *Financial Times*, 15 July 1987.
13 *Paying for Local Government: Summary of the Response to the Green Paper in England*, House of Commons Paper NS 2643.

Chapter 2

Abolishing domestic rates

How good is the government's case for rejecting domestic rates? The Green Paper[1] outlines three principles which a local tax should meet: technical adequacy, fairness and local accountability. It is on the basis of failure to meet these criteria that domestic rates are to be abandoned and the poll tax installed in their place.

How does the present system work?

Local government is financed by a combination of rates, central government grants and its own charges. Rates are a property tax, levied by local authorities themselves, on residential, commercial and industrial property, and on public sector institutions such as hospitals and schools. A rate is made up of two elements — the rate poundage, which is the tax rate, and the rateable value of the property (the hypothetical rent if the property were let in the free market). In England and Wales, rateable values have not been reassessed since 1973 and are therefore very out of date.

Fairness

The government's case
The government admits that rates pass the test of *technical adequacy*. (A local tax is technically adequate if it is cost-effective, fits in with the overall national tax system, allows proper financial control and yields a predictable revenue.) However, rates, it is argued, are unfair. The government measures fairness by the *beneficial* principle and the *redistributive* principle. The former means that the cost of a service is shared out according to who benefits from the service; and the latter means that the cost is shared according to the ability to pay for that service.

The government argues that domestic rates fail to meet the beneficial principle on two grounds. First, they take no account of differences in the size of households (so a single person could be paying the same rates as a couple with three children if they live in properties with the same rateable value); and secondly, they take

10

no account of who consumes which local authority services in what quantities.

Domestic rates also fail the test of redistribution, as they fall more heavily on the poor than on the rich. As no tax can meet both the beneficial and the redistributive principles at the same time, according to the Green Paper, the answer is to plump for the former. The poll tax, in the government's eyes, embodies the beneficial principle; it is to be seen as a *charge* for the use of local services — hence the term 'community charge'.

The counter argument

The case against rates is not water-tight. Starting with the beneficial principle, whilst it is true that rates do not accurately reflect the size of a household, in general the size of property is a fairly good indicator of family size. The most obvious situation where this is not the case is where an elderly person is left alone in the family house.

Secondly, it is very difficult to identify who benefits from what local government services on an individual basis. The benefits or services provided by central and local government, such as the health service, education, transport, and the police force, cannot be apportioned to the individual taxpayer. This is because they are *common* benefits rather than *individual* benefits. Common services supplied by local government are no different from those provided by central government; but, interestingly enough, no one has suggested financing central government by a poll tax.

The government has undertaken no research into what the relationship is between payment of a *local tax* and consumption of services. Even if it were possible to identify a relationship between the tax paid and certain services consumed, all the evidence goes to show that the poll tax would hit the wrong people. As George Jones and Tony Travers point out,[2] young single people, who are heavily hit under the proposals (see Chapter 5) consume few local authority services, while families with children and the elderly, who are less heavily hit, are high users of local authority services. The beneficial principle is not, therefore, a suitable foundation for a local tax.

As for the redistributive principle, the government itself has seriously undermined the progressive element of rates. Rate rebates, given through housing benefit (a benefit to help people on low incomes with the cost of their rates and rents), have been severely cut back in recent years. Since the introduction of housing benefit in 1983, expenditure on the scheme has been reduced by £233m, 1.4m people no longer receive housing benefit, and a further 3.75m receive reduced housing benefit.

11

Secondly, while rates do not neatly correlate with income, the government's own figures[3] show that 83% of people earning £50 per week and below live in properties with average or below average rateable values, while 75% of households with an income of £300 plus per week live in properties with above average rateable values. For the *majority* of households there is a relationship, even if not a very tight one, between income and rate payment.

Thirdly, rates, as a property tax, can be seen in part as a wealth tax — indeed, that was their historical origin. Redistribution is not only about income, but also about wealth.

Local accountability

The government's case

'Local accountability' is defined by the government as establishing a link between eligibility to vote, receipt of local authority services and payment for those services. Domestic rates, it is argued, fail to meet this test of local accountability. First, the tax base (ie, the number of people who pay the tax) is narrow. Of the 35 million electors in England, only 18 million are liable for rates in their own name. Secondly, not everyone bears the full cost of their rates. Only two-thirds, or 12 million, of those who are liable for rates pay them in full. A further 3 million only pay rates in part and another 3 million receive full rebates. 'For those who receive only partial help, the rebates damp the effect of increased local authority spending. And under the present arrangements those who receive full relief can vote for higher services without having to pay anything towards them.'[4]

There is, therefore, a sizeable proportion of electors who do not pay for the services they receive, and for which they may have voted, because they have not been billed directly or because they receive rate rebates.

Thirdly, even for those who do pay rates, it is argued that there is no clear relationship between the rates that they pay and the level of local authority expenditure, due to the operation of the non-domestic rate and the grant system.

The counter argument

The argument that rates fail to meet the test of 'local accountability' can be challenged at a number of levels. First, it is misleading to say that the tax base is narrow. While only 12 million people actually pay rates themselves, there are many other household members, such as the 9½ million spouses/partners of ratepayers, who consider themselves liable for rates, even if they do not receive a bill in their own name. Secondly, people who receive

12

rebates still consider themselves to be ratepayers. The Widdicombe Report states:

> Our own survey of public attitudes suggests that the linkage between voting and paying rates might not be quite as poor as the figures quoted...would suggest. When asked whether or not their household pays rates 94% of electors said 'yes' and only 4% 'no'. This indicates two things. First most electors who do not themselves pay rates are members of a household that does. Second many electors perceive of themselves (or their households) as 'ratepayers' even where their rates are partially or wholly rebated. It was only through a subsequent more detailed question that our survey was able to discover that many of the 94% receive rebates, and even then this was probably understated by the respondents.[5]

In addition, many of those who do not pay rates or who receive rate rebates in full or in part contribute to local authority finance through general taxation. A high proportion of local authority revenue comes, and will continue to come, through central government grants financed by general taxation. While someone who receives a rate rebate might not be a taxpayer at that particular time, she or he will probably have paid income tax previously and will also pay taxes on goods in the shops through VAT. Financial 'accountability' need not operate *only* through payment of rates. It is a distortion to see this group of people as simply parasites on local authorities.

Thirdly, while it is true that there is no clear relationship between the level of rates paid and local authority expenditure, this will be equally true under the new system (see p 29).

More importantly and more generally, in the government's view, 'local accountability' is defined only in *financial* terms rather than as a *democratic* relationship between the voter and his or her representatives.

'Local accountability' is not derived solely from the current ability to pay for services. The logical extension of such a view is that *only* those who pay income tax have a right to vote. This would effectively disenfranchise all groups who pay no income tax, such as many old age pensioners and young people, women who pay no income tax, and the low paid who fall below the tax threshold. Nobody has argued that income tax should be extended to all in the name of *central* accountability. Indeed, government ministers often speak of the need to lift the low-paid out of tax altogether. The term 'local accountability' has undergone a strange redefinition in the government's hands.

'Local accountability' should mean that local representatives are

13

accountable to voters for what they do. For the government, the term means that the voter is accountable for what she or he does at the voting booth — ie, the voter is held to account for voting for services which incur local authority expenditure. At the heart of this view lies the government's belief that the poor should not vote for services unless they also pay for them. The assumption is that, if the poor had explicitly to pay for services, they would not be so keen to vote for them. But voting, it can be argued, is a fundamental political right irrespective of ability to pay. The mechanism for paying for local authority services is a separate question, about the best way of collecting revenue to meet the cost of services — 'best' meaning fairest, most efficient and most effective.

Summary

The government has argued that domestic rates fail the test of fairness, by breaching the beneficial and redistributive principles, and the test of local accountability. However, it has been argued that the beneficial principle is not a suitable basis for a local tax because common benefits and services cannot be attributed to individual taxpayers. While rates are not a progressive tax, there is a broad relationship between rates and income. As for local accountability, the tax base is not as narrow as the government assumes and people who receive rate rebates still contribute to local authority finance through general taxation. More importantly, 'local accountability' has undergone a transformation in the government's hands — it is local *electors*, it seems, rather than local *representatives*, who are to be held to account for voting for increased local authority spending.

References

1 Green Paper, *Paying for Local Government*, Cmnd 9714, HMSO, 1986.
2 *Financial Times*, 15 July 1987.
3 See Green Paper (note 1 above), annex F3.
4 Green Paper (note 1 above), para 1.37.
5 The Widdicombe Report, Cmnd 9797, HMSO, 1986, para 2.78.

Chapter 3

A simple guide to the poll tax

The proposed changes

The poll tax is only one element of three in the government's proposals for the reform of local authority finance:

1. The replacement of domestic rates by a poll tax, a flat-rate charge levied locally on each adult aged 18 and above.

2. The introduction of a uniform business rate set separately for Scotland, England and Wales to replace the locally set non-domestic rate. It will be fixed by central government at the same rate for all non-domestic ratepayers, uprated in line with the retail price index, and distributed to local authorities according to the number of adults in each local authority area.

3. The reform of the central grant system, by replacing the *block grant* (which equalises between authorities for variations in spending needs and rateable resources per head) and the *domestic rate relief grant* (a flat-rate poundage reduction for households) with a new *'Revenue Support Grant'*. This new Revenue Support Grant will consist of (i) grant to equalise variations in expenditure needs, and (ii) grant paid out at a flat rate multiplied by the number of adults in the area.

How will the proposals be phased in?

They will be introduced in Scotland in 1989, and in England and Wales in 1990, with no transition period.

In 13 London local authorities, they will be phased in over four years, to be fully operational in April 1994. In those London authorities, the poll tax will be set initially at £100 in 1990, if local authority spending is the same as in 1989. For four years, they will collect both rates and the poll tax; but any increase in local authority spending will have to come from the poll tax.

To prevent huge shifts in local authority sources of revenue from the changes to the non-domestic rate and central grant system, a 'safety net' will operate. In the first year of the new scheme, the amount of revenue raised from the uniform business rate and new Revenue Support Grant will be the same amount as from the non-domestic rates and government grants under the last year of the present system. Thereafter, this amount will be stepped down over four years (in parallel with the phasing out of domestic rates in England) until it is completely removed.

Who will pay?

Nearly everyone aged 18 and over living in the UK, except in Northern Ireland. Foreigners living in the UK will be liable. Travellers will be liable. Rebates for 80% of poll tax payments will be available through housing benefit; but everyone (bar the exempted categories) will have to pay at least 20% of the poll tax (see p 29). The only people who will *not* have to pay are:

- people under 19 and still at school
- convicted prisoners
- long-term hospital in-patients
- severely mentally disabled people.

Buildings such as hospitals and residential care homes, etc, will be exempt only where the whole of their space is used for people who are exempted from the poll tax. Live-in hospital staff and caretakers, etc, will be liable for the poll tax individually.

What types of poll tax are there?

The *personal poll tax:* this is the flat-rate charge set by each local authority payable by most individuals.

The *standard poll tax:* this is the flat-rate charge on owners or tenants of second homes (and all other domestic properties in which there are no registered personal poll tax payers) (see p 17).

The *collective poll tax:* this is paid by owners or landlords of houses in multi-occupation or short-term occupation (see pp 17-18).

How is the poll tax calculated?

It is calculated by taking total local authority expenditure and deducting central government grant and the uniform business rate; the resulting total is then divided by the number of people liable to pay the poll tax.

The proposals will mean increased *central* control of local government income. The table below shows the proportion of local authority finance controlled by central government under the present and future systems. In England, local authorities will be responsible for raising income to cover only 25% of net spending, in Scotland 20% and in Wales 15%. This will mean that, if

16

local authority spending increases by 1%, the poll tax will have to go up by 3.4% in England and 5.6% in Wales.

Proportion of local authority finance controlled by central government

	Present system	Future system
England	44%	75%
Wales	65%	85%
Scotland	55%	80%

(Source: *Labour Research*, September 1987)

Figures published by the Department of the Environment based on the financial year 1987/8 show that, if the proposals had been fully implemented in 1987/8, the notional level for the poll tax would have been £178 per person.[1] This figure is supposed to allow the *average* council to provide standard services. A poll tax above or below this level is supposed to indicate whether the local authority is a 'low' or 'high' spender. Local authorities which spend over the government targets will have their poll tax capped in the same way as rates have been capped.

Under legislation introducing the poll tax, it is planned that local authorities will have to provide certain types of information about their rate/poll tax demands. All local authorities will be obliged to send out a bill showing by how much they are exceeding government spending limits and what the Department of the Environment thinks the rate/poll tax should be. The intent is to make local authorities carry the blame for increased rates/poll tax rather than central government.

Where is the poll tax paid?

People will be liable for the poll tax in the district or borough where they have their main home. If they have a second home they will pay in addition an amount equivalent to between one and two personal poll taxes, known as the *standard* poll tax, in the area of the second home. This standard poll tax will not be eligible for rebate.

What happens to hotels, hostels and bed and breakfast accommodation?

Hotels catering only for tourists will be commercially rated and residents will not have to pay the poll tax. For bed and breakfast hotels catering for the homeless, the property will not be commercially rated and individual residents will be liable for the poll tax.

17

For hotels that have 'mixed usage', ie, with both long-stay residents and tourists, part of the building will be commercially rated and part registered for the poll tax.

For hostels and other institutions with a large transient population, for whom the institution will, temporarily, be their main residence, there will be a *collective* poll tax. The collective poll tax will be calculated by taking the personal poll tax for the area and multiplying it by the number of people who would normally reside there over a fixed period. This will be payable by the owners or managers and be recoverable from tenants. (The exact definition of a hostel had not been worked out at the time of writing.)

Will caravan or holiday let homes be liable?

Holiday homes and all other temporary homes will be liable for the standard poll tax.

How will the bills for the poll tax work?

The bill will go out, as at present, at the end of March for the following financial year. Payments will largely be by instalments, unless individuals offer to pay otherwise. District and county poll taxes will be combined in a single bill and collection will fall on the authority which collects rates now. Council tenants will be sent a separate poll tax bill (rather than the arrangement at present, where the rates charge is part of the rent demand).

What happens when people move?

The old and the new local authority must be informed. Refunds will be available if the address changes before the financial year is over.

How will the poll tax be collected?

Each local authority will keep a poll tax register separate from the electoral register, although the electoral register can be used for checking purposes. The local authority will be responsible for the cost and maintenance of the poll tax register. A poll tax registration officer will check the register throughout the year. Use of local services, school and social services records, house sales, etc, will be used to cross-check and to keep the register up to date. A canvass of the area will start in the summer of 1989. (It has already begun in Scotland.) Each house will have a 'responsible person' who will be expected to fill in details of all the persons living there. Each individual has a responsibility to ensure that he or she is registered for the poll tax.

18

What penalties apply?

Failure to fill in a canvass form will be a civil offence with a fine of £50. If an individual fails to register, he or she will be liable to (a) the poll tax retrospectively from the time he or she moved into the area, and (b) to an automatic penalty of £50, or 30% of the poll tax, whichever is the higher.

What happens to people who do not pay?

As under the rating system, a local authority will have the power to issue: a reminder to pay; a summons for non-payment through the magistrates' court; and a distress warrant which allows bailiffs to seize goods. In the final instance, non-payment means imprisonment. There has been some suggestion that arrears could be directly deducted from earnings.[2]

Will the register be open to the public?

Individuals will be allowed to examine the whole of their own entry, as will local authority officers, who are responsible for administering the poll tax. *But* the general public will not be able to identify who lives where.

How will married couples be treated?

Husbands and wives will receive individual bills, but will be jointly and severally liable for each other's poll tax. If one defaults, the local authority will be able to take action against the other. If the husband or wife refuses to pay, the partner will be potentially liable for penalties, removal of property and attachment of earnings for non-payment. The government has already indicated that, in Scotland at least, it will treat cohabiting couples, but not separated couples, in the same way. (The cohabitation rule in the present social security system brings intrusive investigation by DHSS officials into whether two people living together constitute a couple; the proposal to make cohabiting couples jointly liable will carry similar dangers.)

Will students be liable for the poll tax?

Students will be liable for 20% of the poll tax in the area in which they study. (It is not yet clear whether there will be any compensation in the grant or whether students will be eligible for rebates.) People on training schemes such as YTS, apprenticeships and traineeships will be liable for the full poll tax, although they would be entitled to rebates.

Are visitors to this country liable for the poll tax?

Visitors will not be liable unless the visit becomes a long stay. (The definition of a long stay is not yet clear.)

What happens to water rates?

It is still unclear how water will be charged for under the proposals. If the privatisation of water goes ahead, and with it water metering, water will eventually be paid for according to how much water is used. (This method of charging for water could hit low income families very hard.[3]) Recently, however, it has been suggested that all adults may be liable for a second poll tax for water; this could increase the average poll tax bill by about 30%.[4]

Will there be charges for local authority services?

A review of local authority charges has been initiated. The Green Paper proposed that the scope of services for which local authorities charge should be widened and existing controls on charges relaxed. This carries clear dangers of hitting the poorest sections of society who are most dependent on some local authority services.[5]

What happens to people on low incomes?

The passing of the Social Security Act 1986 (fully implemented in April 1988) has raised a large number of questions about how the poll tax will interact with the social security system. Details are still being settled at the time of writing.[6]

It was under the Social Security Act that, in the name of 'local accountability', the government proposed that everyone, including those on the very lowest incomes, should pay 20% of their domestic rates without compensation. (At present, anyone on supplementary benefit has the full cost of their rates met.) With the introduction of the poll tax, the requirement to pay 20% of domestic rates would have become a requirement to pay 20% of the poll tax, again without compensation.

However, forced to bow to political pressure in the pre-election period, the government announced in May 1987 that there would indeed be compensation for people on certain social security benefits. At one blow, the government lost £300m of its planned cuts in the reform of social security. So it is not surprising that, in the cooler climate following the election, there has been some rapid rethinking.

How real is the 'compensation'?

Compensation is to take the form of uprating the benefit rate (called personal allowances) for income support (what used to be supplementary benefit), family credit (family income supplement) and housing benefit by 20% of the average domestic rate paid by income support/supplementary benefit claimants. Under the poll tax, this will become 20% of the average poll tax paid in the country (see below).

It is interesting to see what happened in the latest social security uprating announcement as a lesson for the future. When the benefit rates for April 1988 were announced in October 1987, the government said that it had included an average amount of compensation for the 20% contribution to domestic rates (of £1.00 and £1.30 per week) in the personal allowances for income support. Meanwhile, by sleight of hand, it cut the overall level of the personal allowances for income support. It also announced a cut in housing benefit, which will mean that fewer people will be entitled to housing benefit, and therefore to the 'compensation', in the first place.

Beneath these obscure technicalities there is an important point. 'Compensation' is clearly a nonsense if at the same time the overall benefit level is being cut. While the government refuses to publish a breakdown of how it constructs the personal allowances for income support (ie, what amount is attributable to, say, fuel, food, domestic rates, etc), it is impossible to identify whether the promise of 'compensation' is real. The lesson for the future is clear — promises of 'compensation' should be treated very cautiously.

How will the poll tax rebates work?

Everyone, including claimants, will have to pay at least 20% of the poll tax (see page 16 for exceptions). For people on income support, family credit or housing benefit there will be 'compensation' in their benefit. Claimants in turn will have to pay out their 20% to the local authority. This 'compensation' will be 20% of the *average* poll tax paid for the country. Therefore the compensation will not cover the full costs for people living in areas with a poll tax higher than the average.

Unlike the present housing benefit scheme, which is based on rates paid by the whole *household*, poll tax rebates will be on an *individual* basis. Each individual will be eligible for his or her own rebate. There will be no non-dependant deductions in the poll tax rebate scheme (deductions made from housing benefit for sons and daughters in work, grandparents and some lodgers, who are assumed to be contributing to the household's housing costs) because non-dependants will, of course, themselves be paying the poll tax. Couples will have their rebates assessed jointly, although there might be the option of choosing which partner should receive the rebate. Partners of people exempted from the poll tax, such as students, will be assessed for rebate separately. Tenants who pay the collective poll tax, ie, those in hostels, will be eligible for

21

rebates on their poll tax contributions in the same way as the personal poll tax rebate is calculated.

When the poll tax and rates are running in tandem, there will have to be some kind of double rebate scheme. At present the DHSS is considering developing a transitional combined poll tax/rates rebate scheme. The details of such a complex scheme have yet to be worked out. Local authorities will continue to receive a direct subsidy for a large part of the costs of rebates and the administration of the rebate scheme. However, the level and adequacy of such subsidies may well continue to be a source of controversy and friction between central and local government.

References

1 *House of Commons Hansard*, 29 June 1987.
2 *House of Commons Hansard*, 24 July 1987, col 722.
3 See *Response to Proposals to Extend Water Metering*, CPAG, 1986.
4 *The Guardian*, 20 October 1987.
5 See *A Feudal Levy*, CPAG, 1986.
6 See Paper for the Housing Benefit Standing Committee, 428N/CC, 3 September 1987.

Chapter 4

What's wrong with the poll tax?

There has been widespread and serious criticism of the poll tax. The discussion here is organised around four central issues: technical adequacy, fairness, and local accountability (the government's own criteria for a good tax) — and, in addition, the impact of the poll tax on the poorest, those on social security.

Technical adequacy

A major hurdle for the poll tax is the test of technical adequacy. It has been estimated by the government that the cost of administering the poll tax would be twice that of administering the rates (simply because twice as many people will pay the poll tax as currently pay rates).[1] The Chartered Institute of Public Finance and Accountancy (CIPFA) has estimated that the interim costs of operating the poll tax and rates in tandem will be four times the present cost of administering the rates. The Rating and Valuation Association has put a figure of £40m on preparation for the poll tax and has estimated that preparation will require 10,000 new jobs. The same organisation has also said that the administrative cost of collecting the 20% contribution from the poorest claimants will outweigh any financial gain from the contributions themselves.[2] Cheapness of the cost of collecting a tax is clearly an important criterion for government. The poll tax does not score well on this particular test. All commentators agree that there will be major difficulties in implementing the poll tax.

1. Taxing a mobile population

It is far easier to tax property than people. Fifteen per cent of the population moves house in a year. In some inner cities 25% move in a year. Losses could amount to £500m a year through people not being billed for the poll tax. The expense and difficulty of administration have a knock-on effect. Jeff Pipe, a Birmingham City Treasurer, estimated that the poll tax might yield 25% less than expected because of incomplete records and evasion. This will immediately mean bigger bills for those who are paying, possibly creating even more reluctance to pay the tax. Gordon Hughes has estimated that in Scotland the average poll tax would be £6.62 per week in 1988 if there were a 100% collection rate; this rises to £7.33 with a 90% collection rate, and to £8.19 with an 80% collection rate.[3]

2. Using the electoral register to check the poll tax register
The freedom to use the electoral register to cross-check the poll tax register will undoubtedly mean that some people will not register to vote. As it is, a high proportion of people in inner cities do not return their electoral registration forms. About 1.3 million people could not vote in the last general election because their names were not on the register. In areas of inner London, up to 17% of people are not on the register.[4]

The higher the poll tax, the more incentive there will be for people, particularly those on low incomes, to disenfranchise themselves. As Brian Reading writes in the *Sunday Times*, 'The tax will inevitably create a ghostly army of "no fixed abode" who prefer to disenfranchise themselves rather than pay. Anyone hiding from the poll tax will hardly register for the vote. The poll tax will become equivalent to a property or means qualification for voting as poll taxes were for blacks in America's southern states after the civil war. So a new tax principle is being established in Britain—no representation without taxation.'[5]

So it will be the poor and the mobile and the inner city population who will be disenfranchised — a far cry from 'local accountability'. This can be seen as a form of gerrymandering. The people most tempted to evade the poll tax by not registering on the electoral roll will be the poorest — perhaps those least likely to vote Conservative!

3. Collecting names for the poll tax register from those making use of local authority services
This would obviously act as a disincentive to using local authority services such as libraries, swimming pools, lunch clubs and community centres. Again, this could hit the poorest hardest as they are often the most reliant on many of those services.

4. Difficulties of constructing a test of residence
It is very unclear how this will work. When will a long visit turn into residence? Any test of residence carries with it the risk of racial discrimination. Will anyone who is black be harassed because it will be assumed that he or she is a visitor, rather than a resident of this country?

5. A centralised computerised record for the poll tax could easily be misused There has been some suggestion that a poll tax register would inevitably be computerised. This could very easily be misused. The Data Protection Registrar has produced a report expressing concern about individual privacy.[6] A report by the Commission for Racial Equality found that people decided not to register on the electoral roll because of the fears of nationality checks, being chased up for unpaid debts, and violence from former husbands or boyfriends.[7] How are these concerns going to be met under a public poll tax register?

As the local government minister himself has said, there will be 'no place to hide' from the poll tax. An identity numbering system is already being compiled in Scotland. As a National Council for Civil Liberties report argues, the poll tax brings with it a serious invasion of privacy: files will be cross-checked; people's movements will be monitored; and officials will be under pressure to collect information. While individuals will have the right to see their entry on the register, they will not have the power to change that entry.[8]

The Rating and Valuation Association has also expressed concern about the implications for individual privacy: 'The introduction of an official inspectorate to track down these missing millions will be expensive and inevitably intrusive. . . Without an army of snoopers or an official identity system it will not be possible to locate the missing millions already not on the register of electors.'[9]

Is the poll tax register the first step towards a society where everyone will have to carry an identity card? As Conservative MP Sir Philip Goodhart said: 'It will be ironic if it is found that a whole new system of personal identification has to be introduced in order to provide an administrative base for collecting a community charge.'[10]

The practical problems dismissed so lightly in the Green Paper pose major problems for the poll tax. The earlier Green Paper, *Alternatives to Rates*, published in 1981 (Cmnd 8449), rejected the poll tax partly on administrative grounds. The government is no longer heeding its own advice.

Fairness

'The Conservative manifesto for the last election promised to replace the domestic rate with a "fairer community charge". It is because I and many of my colleagues in the Conservative Party do not believe that the present proposals for a poll tax are fair that we are so strongly opposed to them.'
(The Rt Hon Edward Heath MP, *The Times*, 17 July 1987)

25

The government argues that the poll tax will mean that the amount of local taxation paid will be more closely related to the use of local authority services. However, as argued earlier (p 11), the 'beneficial principle' is not an adequate basis for a local tax. In relation to the 'redistributive principle', the government argues that the poll tax is no more regressive than rates. However, the terms of the debate are falsely drawn.

In the Green Paper's analysis of the options for reforming local government finance,[11] the poll tax is compared to the present rates system, which is universally regarded as far from perfect. There is no consideration of what might be achieved by reforming the rating system as an option. So the poll tax proposals are not considered in their own right but in comparison with an already inadequate and unsatisfactory system of local taxation.

The whole question of whether a local tax should be more closely related to income is evaded, by arbitrarily hiving off the uncomfortable problems of poverty and low income into the social security system: 'The Government considers that it would be better for there to be an explicit income support scheme operated through the social security system than to obscure the true costs of the local contribution to services by, for example, having a lower community charge for those with low incomes.'[12] Thus the fairness of the poll tax is simply not addressed; the issue is shunted to one side.

As for the redistributive principle, a flat-rate charge clearly falls more heavily on those with low incomes than on those with high incomes. Even the government's own table shows that the poll tax will be *more regressive* than rates (see Table A).

When comparing the poll tax and rates, adjusting for family size, the poll tax makes up a far lower proportion of net income for those people in the highest income bands. For example, a household with an income of £75-£100 per week pays £5.03 rates per week on average, or 3.7% of net income; this rises to £5.32 under the poll tax, or 3.9% of net income. At the other end of the income scale, a household with an income of £500 or more per week pays £12.48 rates per week, or 1.8% of net income; this falls by nearly half to £6.64 under the poll tax, or 1.0% of net income.

While the table shows that rates, too, are regressive, it is clear that the poll tax is even more so. As the example above shows, *a family with an income of £75-£100 per week is contributing about four times as much of their net income in the poll tax as a family on £500 plus.* (See Chapter 5 for a fuller analysis.)

The conclusion of the Institute for Fiscal Studies was that: 'The community charge will generally benefit higher income households and at the highest levels of income the benefits will be substantial.

In this respect the community charge will be much more poorly related to ability to pay than are rates.'[13]

Table A *Relationship of rates and the poll tax to net income*

Weekly net equivalent* income	Net rates		Net poll tax	
	£s per week	as a % of net income	£s per week	as a % of net income
Under £50	£1.12	2.1	£1.02	1.9
£50-£75	£2.65	3.3	£2.68	3.3
£75-£100	£5.03	3.7	£5.32	3.9
£100-£150	£5.82	3.2	£6.08	3.3
£150-£200	£6.37	2.8	£6.33	2.8
£200-£250	£6.74	2.6	£6.16	2.4
£250-£300	£7.59	2.6	£6.06	2.1
£300-£350	£8.32	2.5	£6.12	1.9
£350-£400	£9.50	2.5	£6.08	1.6
£400-£500	£10.16	2.3	£6.00	1.4
Over £500	£12.48	1.8	£6.64	1.0
All households	£4.81	3.0	£4.77	3.0

* income adjusted for family size   *(GB, 1984/5 prices)*
(Source: Green Paper, *Paying for Local Government,* Annex F, Fig F5)

It is the fact that the poll tax is, of its very nature, *entirely unrelated to people's ability to pay*, that has attracted such widespread criticism: In Conservative MP Timothy Raison's view: 'Although a system of relief would be built into it for the poor, it still seems inequitable that the richest would be paying no more than the all but poor — the multi-millionaire no more than his maid.'[14] And a *Financial Times* leader stated: 'Simple principles usually make bad law and this proposal is no exception. In trying to relate charges to services, the Conservatives have ignored one of the oldest of all fiscal principles — that taxes should be related to ability to pay. This omission is acceptable for relatively minor charges such as the TV licence. The budget for local services is much too heavy to be paid in this fashion.'[15] The point should also be made that people have the freedom to choose whether to have a television, and therefore a licence; the same choice does not extend to local taxation.

Another aspect of fairness is the relative burden of local tax between households of different sizes, or what is known as horizontal equity. The poll tax falls more heavily on households which contain more than two adults. This is of particular concern for low income families with young adults at home, those who care for elderly or sick people in the home, and ethnic minorities, who are more likely to live in larger households (see Chapter 5).

A side issue, but integral to the question of fairness, is the boost to house prices which will result from the abolition of domestic rates. The government's own figures estimate that the price of housing could increase by as much as 15% in the first instance, settling down to 5% in the longer term.[16] Other estimates by Gordon Hughes in Scotland suggest that the rise could be as much as 25%.[17] As Peter Oppenheimer pointed out in *The Guardian*, the abolition of rates will be a bonus to the owner-occupier because property will effectively be untaxed.[18] This will in turn mean a rise in prices and a less efficient use of space. It is a spur for the affluent to buy oversized second homes at a time when homelessness is soaring. The indirect boost to house prices will be a simple bonus for the rich.

Local accountability

The poll tax fails the test of local accountability even in its own terms.

First, as wives and husbands will be jointly liable for the poll tax, the tax net will not be extended as far as intended. Secondly, many young people, brought into the tax net for the first time, will be dependent on poll tax rebates, thus defeating the government's aim of reducing dependency on rebates (which, it argues, diminishes local accountability).

Thirdly, as argued earlier (see pp 16-17), the financial gearing of the poll tax will increase central government responsibility for the financing of local government. Any marginal increase in local authority spending falls on the poll tax. Rises in local spending might be for any number of reasons — the local authority may choose to spend on different priorities from those of central government; or inflation may be higher than expected; or the local authority's needs may be assessed wrongly by central government. But any spending above the national average pattern is heavily penalised, because it falls so heavily on the local electorate. For every £1 rise in local authority spending, the poll tax will rise by roughly £4. This is a *distorted* accountability — one which weighs most heavily on those with the lowest incomes.

But, as Tony Wilson writes, the need to make choices about how far to depart from average spending is one of the main reasons for having local government. The case against too much centralisation of local authority finance rests on two points: 'The first is the familiar case... for some measure of autonomy for local government

— real autonomy, not just a formal freedom that could be exercised only at unacceptable cost. The second is that the government is implicitly expressing vast confidence in *its* ability to assess local needs.'[19]

Clearly the intention is to use the poll tax as a tool for greater control of local government expenditure. When Nicholas Ridley published figures showing the high level of the poll tax in inner city areas, he said that the figures 'clearly illustrate the importance of high spending authorities starting now to identify economies and those who live in those authorities insisting that they do so.'[20]

Research by CIPFA has shown that, contrary to government claims, there is no simple link between local authority spending and the level of the poll tax. The level of the poll tax is determined by three factors: population, central government grant and local spending. It is the interdependence of these factors which weakens the link between changes in spending and the level of the poll tax. Their research on what the situation would have been if the poll tax was in effect now found there was not one local authority in England where the change in spending would have equalled the change in the level of the poll tax. In 29 local authorities, the poll tax would have risen while spending per adult fell; in 21 local authorities, the poll tax would have fallen although spending per adult rose. CIPFA comments:

> It is somewhat disturbing that for some authorities community charges would have risen even though spending fell; and that for others community charges would have fallen even though spending rose. Movements of this kind must challenge the argument underlying the Green Paper that the new proposals would 'considerably improve the accountability of local authorities to their electors for their expenditure and taxation decisions'. These movements also bring into question the statement that the 'reasons for increases in local taxes will be clearer'.[21]

The poll tax and the poor

The government's case for compelling everyone to pay 20% towards their rates/poll tax was that in the interests of 'local accountability' everyone should make some contribution regardless of ability to pay. This was softened by the promise to pay average 'compensation' by raising the level of income support, family credit and housing benefit appropriately (see p 21). Even if this promise were fully implemented, all social security claimants living in areas with above average poll tax will be worse off, some by considerable amounts — although social security claimants living in areas where the poll tax is below the average may, of course, be better off.

Norman Tebbit has made clear the intention behind this averaging out of compensation: 'If the person concerned lives in a good Tory borough, where things are well managed, their average amount will more than pay their community charge. If they live in one of the less happy boroughs, they may find it's rather more difficult. But that is a decision of the local authority — whether it overcharges them or not.'[22] As this quotation makes clear, there is a political target. Claimants will find cuts in their benefits which may push them below what the government deems to be the national minimum income for those who are not in full-time work, ie, the income support (previously supplementary benefit) level. It seems plausible to assume (in the absence of adequate research) that social security claimants are more likely to be concentrated in areas such as inner cities and the North and North-East, where unemployment is very high (see Chapter 5), where the poll tax will be well above average. If this is so, far more social security claimants will lose than gain. Thus, in seeking to punish errant Labour authorities, the government will simply punish the poorest households. As Ronald Butt in *The Times* wrote: 'Is it fair to penalise, say, a single parent with three children on social security, who happens to live in Camden, compared with her equivalent in Wimbledon? What will be the public response if she suddenly defaults; will the local authority distrain her goods or eventually have her sent to jail?'[23]

The mechanism for poll tax 'compensation' has to be placed in the context of the social security reforms to be implemented fully in April 1988. The introduction of the social fund (which replaces with loans most one-off lump sum grants for cookers, furniture, etc) will push many claimants even further into debt. It is going to be very difficult for people on the lowest incomes operating within very tight budgets to put aside the allocated amount (if there is any) for the payment of their poll tax. This will obviously be far worse for people who do not receive the full 'compensation'. The shortfall in poll tax 'compensation' for people living in areas with above average poll tax will only add to the mounting debt problems already likely to be experienced.

The government has chosen a faulty mechanism for increasing 'local accountability' at the cost of providing an even more inadequate income for the poorest in our society. Sir George Young has commented: 'The argument that this transaction is going to rekindle a new interest in municipal affairs and persuade lifelong Labour voters to vote Conservative is ridiculous.'[24] And: 'Billions of pounds will be churned in this exercise, being inserted into the pockets of the poor by central government and extracted hours later by local government. But for hundreds of thousands of the poorest, the 20% they get from the government will not cover the actual 20% rates [or community charge] due in their town hall, leaving them up to £8 a week worse off.'[25]

Apart from the hardship that the proposal will create, there are a number of other problems. First, there is the administrative cost of collecting small contributions to the poll tax. Secondly, the caseload and the cost of housing benefit will increase because individuals rather than households will pay the poll tax. The Green Paper estimates that there will be an 18% increase in claims — ie, 1.2 million new cases — and an increase of £100m, or 4%, in expenditure. The well-documented chaos that accompanied the introduction of housing benefit in 1982/3 means that even now some local authorities are only just managing their caseloads. The increase in housing benefit claims could mean that even more claimants experience long delays before receiving their benefits.

There has been no mention of the problem of low take-up of housing benefit. The latest figures, for 1984, show that 77% of those eligible claimed housing benefit.[26] Housing benefit has been subject to enormous cuts since its introduction, on the grounds that too many people are receiving it and that the expenditure is too high. The scenario is only too clear: the poll tax will push many more people on to housing benefit, causing increased expenditure; increased dependency and higher expenditure then become the justification for further cuts in the benefit levels, leaving more people exposed to poverty.

Thirdly, the extension of housing benefit to many people who were not on means-tested benefits before is a widening of the poverty trap. As Hermione Parker wrote in *The Times:*

> The poll tax will extend the resulting tax induced poverty trap to a previously unaffected, but particularly vulnerable section of the community — young single people entering the regular job market...pauperising people whose income would otherwise be sufficient, charging them tax they cannot afford to pay and then expecting them to claim the tax back through all manner of income tested benefits. First they are robbed of their earnings and then of their self-esteem.[27]

Summary

As we have seen, the poll tax brings in its wake intractable problems. It will be difficult and costly to administer; provides a direct incentive for people not to vote and use local authorities services; and has worrying implications for civil liberties. As a tax entirely

31

unrelated to people's ability to pay, the poll tax will be far more regressive than rates. In addition, the poll tax will create a distorted 'accountability', whereby an extra pound spent by the local authority falls four times as heavily on the electorate. It is those on the lowest incomes who have to bear the cost of this financial gearing. When it comes to social security, the decision to 'compensate' social security claimants for the national *average* poll tax will mean severe losses for claimants living in areas with a high poll tax. The government's dogged determination to force 'high spending' local authorities to reduce their expenditure is at the expense of the poorest citizens.

References

1 *House of Commons Hansard*, 6 July 1987, col 57.
2 *Community Charge/Poll Tax: The Facts*, Rating and Valuation Association, September 1987.
3 Gordon Hughes, *Community Charge, At What Cost?*, Scottish Local Government Unit, 1987.
4 *Electoral Registration in Inner Cities 1983-4*, HMSO, 1987.
5 *Sunday Times*, 19 July 1987.
6 *The Guardian*, 16 July 1987.
7 M J Le Lohe, *A study of non-registration among ethnic minorities*, CRE, 1987.
8 *The Privacy Implications of the Poll Tax*, NCCL, 1987.
9 See note 2.
10 *Daily Telegraph*, 1 August 1987.
11 Green Paper, *Paying for Local Government*, Cmnd 9714, HMSO, 1986.
12 Green Paper (note 11), para 3.45.
13 S Smith and D Squire, *Who will be paying for Local Government?*, IFS, 1987.
14 *The Times*, 29 July 1987.
15 *Financial Times*, leader, 29 May 1987.
16 Green Paper (note 11), annex E.
17 *Oxford Review of Economic Policy*, Summer 1987.
18 *The Guardian*, 3 October 1987.
19 T Wilson, 'Paying for local government', *Policy Studies*, Autumn 1986.
20 *House of Commons Hansard*, 29 June 1987, col 44.
21 Chartered Institute of Public Finance and Accountancy (CIPFA), *Paying for Local Government, Beyond the Green Paper, Update*, August 1987. This research was based on the central government grant reforms initially proposed in the Green Paper. The government has subsequently altered the proposals, but CIPFA maintains that there will still be no obvious relationship between local authority expenditure and the level of the poll tax.
22 *The Independent*, 23 May 1987.
23 *The Times*, 25 June 1987.
24 *The Times*, 22 July 1987.
25 *The Guardian*, 14 September 1987.
26 *Housing Benefit Take-Up Technical Note*, DHSS Statistics and Research Division, May 1987.
27 *The Times*, 25 July 1987.

Chapter 5

Who will lose?

The overhaul of local government finance will mean far-reaching changes for individuals, for local authorities, and for regions. There have been a number of different assessments of the likely effects.

The overall picture

The government's own estimates* (see Table B) show that when the proposals are fully implemented 10,575,000, or 51%, of households will gain, and 10,000,000, or 49%, will lose. What is the scale of the gains and losses? About 15% of households stand to gain £2-£10 per week and the same proportion stand to lose £2-£10 per week. It should be borne in mind that average weekly rate payments for England and Wales are in fact only about £8 a week;[1] so a loss of £2-£10 is quite considerable.

Table B also shows that the majority of single adult households will gain — 83% of single adult households (including single pensioners) gain from the proposals. The majority of three adult households lose — 85% in fact lose from the proposals.

The difficulty with these figures is that they look at households rather than individuals. An analysis by John Gibson (see Table C) points out that the average number of individuals in households where bills will increase (ie, the losers) is larger than in households where the bills will decrease (ie, the gainers).[2] He reanalyses the government's figures on an individual basis and finds a gloomier picture — 44% of individual electors gain from the changes, but 56% lose. He also shows that the number of large losers (£2 or more a week, or £100 or more a year) far outweighs the number of large gainers. Some 8.3 million people lose £2 plus a week, compared to the 5.2m who gain £2 plus a week.

---

*All estimates contained in this chapter assume the payment of 20% of the poll tax by everyone and make no adjustment for any 'compensation' in the rates of social security for this 20% contribution. At the time of writing, there has been no analysis of the effects of this compensation. As we were going to press, however, new figures were published slightly altering the proportion of overall gainers (from 51% to 55%) and losers (from 49% to 45%). See *House of Commons Hansard*, 26 October 1987, col 36; and 2 November 1987, col 521.

Table B *Households gaining and losing with full replacement of domestic rates by the poll tax — by type of household (GB, thousands, 1984/5 prices)*

£ per week	Single pensioner	Other single	Two adults	Three+ adults	All households
Losers					
10+	—	—	0	50	50
5-10	—	—	75	425	500
2-5	0	75	1,325	1,125	2,525
1-2	25	100	1,625	425	2,175
0-1	375	275	3,750	325	4,725
Total losers	400	475	6,800	2,350	10,000
Gainers					
0-1	1,700	775	2,800	200	5,475
1-2	250	350	1,275	100	1,975
2-5	350	600	1,400	100	2,450
5-10	75	100	350	25	575
10+	25	25	50	0	100
Total gainers	2,400	1,850	5,875	425	10,575

Note: 0 = less than 12,500 households
(Source: Green Paper, *Paying for Local Government,* Cmnd 9714, HMSO, 1986)

Table C *Electors gaining and losing with full replacement of domestic rates by the poll tax (GB, thousands, 1984/5 prices)*

£ per week	Single pensioner	Other single	Two adults	Three+* adults	All households
Losers					
10+	—	—	0	175	175
5-10	—	—	150	1,488	1,638
2-5	0	75	2,650	3,825	6,550
1-2	25	100	3,250	1,445	4,820
0-1	375	275	7,500	1,105	9,255
Total losers	400	475	13,600	8,038	22,438
Gainers					
0-1	1,700	775	5,600	660	8,735
1-2	250	350	2,550	330	3,480
2-5	350	600	2,800	330	4,080
5-10	75	100	700	80	955
10+	25	25	100	0	150
Total gainers	2,400	1,850	11,750	1,400	17,400

*Size of three-adult household assumed to be between 3.2 and 3.5 adults.
(Source: *Public Service and Local Government,* June 1987)

Gainers and losers by income

Losers from the changes are concentrated among those with low incomes (see Table D). Sixty per cent of two-adult households with incomes below £200 lose, compared with 36% of similar households earning £200 plus a week.

Table D *Two-adult households gaining/losing by full replacement of domestic rates by the poll tax (England, thousands, 1984/5 prices)*

£ per week	All income levels	Incomes below £200	Incomes above £200
Total	10,857	7,631	3,255
Losers			
10+	2	1	1
5-10	86	52	34
2-5	1,213	893	320
1-2	1,341	1,006	335
0-1	3,104	2,625	479
Total losers	5,745	4,577	1,169
Gainers			
0-1	2,440	1,857	583
1-2	1,111	649	462
2-5	1,216	491	725
5-10	310	55	255
10+	52	3	49
Total gainers	5,130	3,054	2,086

(Source: *Public Service and Local Government,* July 1987)

It is difficult to measure the overall effect of the poll tax on social security claimants with any accuracy. However, the requirement for everyone to contribute at least 20% to the poll tax, despite the so-called 'compensation' (see p 21), will be a heavy burden on the poorest. In particular, the proposal to reimburse social security claimants by 20% of the national *average* poll tax will mean that people on low incomes in areas where the poll tax will be high (see p 29) — ie, in inner city areas, in particular London — will suffer large drops in their weekly income.

Here is an example of the effect of compensating on an average basis:

For example: Camden poll tax of £782 per year (see p 40)
20% of the poll tax in Camden is £156.40

The national average poll tax is £224
20% of this is £44.80

This leaves a shortfall of £111.60 per year to be paid by a
social security claimant out of his/her benefit.

Gainers and losers by family type

Table E shows how the losses increase with the number of people
in the household: 2% of one-adult households lose 2% or more of
net income, compared to 29% of three-adult households. Pensioner
couples losing far outweigh those who gain: 14% lose 1-2% of net
income and a further 10% lose more than 2% of net income. So
over a fifth of pensioner couples will lose from the proposals.
Although the losses are generally small, they are imposed on many
of those with the lowest incomes. There is a principle at issue. The
broadest backs should bear the costs of change.

Carers for elderly or disabled relatives, mostly women, are more
likely to be living in households with more than two adults. They
are therefore likely to be heavily hit by the poll tax. This is
strangely at odds with the government's community care policy, as
anyone who moves from an institution or residential home will
immediately become liable to the poll tax — a clear deterrent to
the government's favoured policy option.

The other group which is particularly heavily hit by the proposals are young people who are not householders, who are brought
into the tax net for the first time. Using the government figures,
21% of the 52% of tax units who lose will be non-householders. In
combination with a number of other measures, like the removal of
Wages Council protection for workers under the age of 21 and the
lower income support rate for single childless people aged under
25, young people are at the receiving end of some of the harshest
of government policies.

Gainers and losers by rateable value and family size

Table F looks at the interaction of rateable value and family size.
The first column gives the average rateable value in England and
Wales and shows that a one-adult household would gain £201, a
two-adult household would lose £23, a three-adult household
would lose £247, and a four-adult household £471. The larger the
number of adults in the household, the more likely it is to lose
because of the larger number of people who will be paying the poll
tax.

Table E *Percentage of households gaining and losing from replacement of domestic rates by a poll tax*

Percentages of:	Households gaining: more than 2% of net income	between 1% and 2% of net income	Households whose net local tax payments change by less than 1% of net income	Households losing: between 1% and 2% of net income	more than 2% of net income
All households	4	7	66	13	10
One-adult households	14	14	67	4	2
Two-adult households	4	9	67	13	8
Three+ adult households	2	2	40	27	29
Single pensioner households	1	3	94	1	2
Pensioner couples	3	7	67	14	10

(Source: S Smith and Duncan Squire, *Local Taxes and Local Government*, IFS, 1987)

Table F *Likely impact of the poll tax by household size and rateable value (RV) of property in England*

Rateable value bands	*Av England*	*up to £75*	*£75-£100*	*£101-£125*	*£126-£150*	*£151-£400*	*£400*
Average rateable value	£202	£58	£88	£114	£138	£228	£549
Rate bill 1987-88	£425	£122	£185	£240	£290	£480	£1,155
Poll tax 1987-88	£224	£224	£224	£224	£224	£224	£224
Gain or loss:							
1 adult	£201	−£102	−£39	£16	£66	£256	£931
2 adults	−£23	−£326	−£263	−£208	−£158	£32	£707
3 adults	−£247	−£550	−£487	−£432	−£382	−£192	£483
4 adults	−£471	−£774	−£711	−£656	−£606	−£416	£259

(Source: CIPFA: *Paying for Local Government, Beyond the Green Paper, Update* (supplement), 1987)

In low-rated property, the losses for all family types are greater, and even a one-adult household loses. So, for example, a pensioner living on her own in a property rated at £88 would lose £39 per year from the proposals, whilst a couple with a working daughter at home in a property of the same rateable value would lose £487 per year.

The table shows the shift in the burden from those living in homes with a high rateable value to those living in homes with a low rateable value, and from single person households to those with three adults or more. All households with more than two adults will lose unless they are in properties with high rateable values. A single person will gain unless she or he is in a property with a very low rateable value. Because this table is of a typical local authority, it does not show how these family types would fare in different areas. In certain areas such as inner London, where the poll tax will be very high (see next section), even single house-holders and large families in properties with high rateable values will lose.[3]

> Ms McKenzie, a single parent mother with a 6-year-old child, living in Hammersmith and in full-time work, would pay £404 in domestic rates on average in 1987 and would pay £465 under the poll tax — a rise of 15%.

It is only properties with medium to high rateable values where there are gains for the occupants. The important point is that rate-able value is a rough indication of income; so the poorest people in properties with the lowest rateable value lose, while those in properties with the highest rateable values — the richest — gain.

By region

The government has produced its own estimates of the likely level of the poll tax assuming that the reforms were fully in place in 1987/88.[4]

Any comparative analysis of rates and the poll tax is hindered by the fact that rates bills are calculated *per household* while the poll tax is calculated *per individual*. The figures below (Table G), adjusted for comparison, show where the heaviest burden will fall. The metropolitan areas and inner London would experience sharp rises in local tax, while shire areas and outer London boroughs would experience a drop.

Looking more closely at the different regions, Table H shows that the changes will mean a shift in the burden of taxation away

Table G

	Av rate bill per household 1987/8	Av poll tax for 2 adult household 1987/8	% increase/ decrease between av rate and poll tax for 2 adults
England total	£440	£448 (224)	+ 2%
Total shire areas	£419	£384 (192)	- 8%
Total metropolitan areas	£424	£462 (231)	+ 9%
Inner boroughs	£594	£1,114 (557)	+ 88%
Outer boroughs	£517	£452 (226)	- 13%
London total	£546	£696 (348)	+ 28%

(Figures in brackets show the average poll tax per individual)

from the South towards the North, Yorkshire and Humberside. The North experiences a rise in the local tax bill of 31%, and Yorkshire and Humberside a rise of 32%. Meanwhile, in the South East, the local tax bill drops by 23%.

> Mr and Mrs Anderson live in Yorkshire, both in full-time work. They have two children aged 15 and 18. The older one is in full-time work. In 1987, they would pay on average £354 in domestic rates; under the poll tax they would pay a total of £699 (three times an individual poll tax of £233) — a rise of 98%.

Table H

	Av rate bill per household 1987/8	Av poll tax per 2 adult household 1987/8	% increase/ decrease between av rate and poll tax for 2 adults
Northern region	£390	£512 (256)	+ 31%
Yorkshire/Humberside	£354	£466 (233)	+ 32%
North West	£426	£446 (223)	+ 5%
East Midlands	£398	£412 (206)	+ 4%
West Midlands	£442	£366 (183)	- 17%
East Anglia	£382	£344 (172)	- 10%
Greater London	£546	£696 (348)	+ 28%
South East	£479	£368 (184)	- 23%
South West	£389	£372 (186)	+ 4%

> Mr Charles, a computer programmer, living in the South West
> of England, would pay on average £389 in domestic rates in
> 1987; under the poll tax he would pay £186 — a fall of 52%.

Inner London

It is in inner London that the most striking rises occur. The highest
poll tax will be in Camden and the lowest in Kensington and
Chelsea (see Table I).

Table I

	Av rate bill per household	Av poll tax for 2 adult household	% increase/ decrease between av rate bill and poll tax for 2 adults
Inner London			
Camden	£843	£1,564 (782)	+ 86%
Greenwich	£495	£1,216 (608)	+ 146%
Hackney	£765	£1,382 (691)	+ 81%
Hammersmith/Fulham	£404	£930 (465)	+ 130%
Islington	£552	£966 (483)	+ 75%
Kensington/Chelsea	£605	£740 (370)	+ 22%
Lambeth	£536	£1,094 (547)	+ 104%
Lewisham	£684	£1,354 (677)	+ 98%
Southwark	£499	£1,140 (570)	+ 129%
Tower Hamlets	£548	£1,278 (639)	+ 133%
Wandsworth	£399	£870 (435)	+ 118%
Westminster	£811	£792 (396)	− 2%

Ethnic minorities

Black people will be particularly heavily hit by the poll tax. As the
Low Pay Review (Autumn 1987) shows, this is because black
people are more likely to be on lower incomes, live in inner city
areas and belong to larger than average size households.

In 1982, Afro-Caribbean men had earnings of £129.20 per week
and Asian men earnings of £110.70, compared with £129.00 for
white men. The unemployment rate is also much higher for Afro-
Caribbean and Asian people than for white people — in 1985 it

stood at 21% for Afro-Caribbeans, 31% for Pakistanis/Bangladeshis and 10% for whites.

Sixty-eight per cent of people from ethnic minorities lived in the metropolitan counties in 1985, compared with 31% of white people. This is even higher for certain ethnic groups — 80% of Afro-Caribbeans, 75% of Bangladeshis and 71% of Pakistanis lived in metropolitan counties in 1985.

As far as household size is concerned, the Policy Studies Institute found that 6% of whites, 17% of Afro-Caribbeans and 22% of Asians lived in households with more than three adults.[5]

Mr and Mrs Pillay, both in full-time work, live in Tower Hamlets with two school-aged children and an elderly relative on supplementary pension. In 1987, they would pay on average £548 in domestic rates and would have to pay £1,361 in poll tax bills (twice the individual poll tax of £639 and £83 to make up for the shortfall in 'compensation' for the 20% contribution) — a rise of 148%.

As the foregoing has shown, people who are on low incomes, live in inner city areas (in particular London) and are part of larger households will suffer major losses from the introduction of the poll tax. A high proportion of black households are likely to receive some of the highest poll tax bills.

Local profiles

CIPFA has produced tables which show how the poll tax will affect households of different sizes in different local authorities. For example, in Lewisham (see Table J) the average rate is £233. Eighty-nine per cent in the borough live in homes with a rateable value of between £150 and £400. As is clear from the table, it is only in homes with the highest rateable values of £400 plus that a two-adult household would gain. But only 2% of households actually fall into this band.[6]

Summary

The final picture of who gains or loses from the reforms is a product of the complex interaction of a number of factors: whether the local authority is a 'high' or 'low' spender; how dependent the local authority is on non-domestic rates for its revenue; the rateable value of domestic property and the number

Table J Likely impact of the poll tax by household size and rateable value (RV) of property in Lewisham

Rateable value bands		up to £75	£75-£100	£101-£125	£126-£150	£151-£400	£400
Average rateable value	£233	£18	£94	£117	£138	£240	£468
	£	£	£	£	£	£	£
Rate bill 1987-88	513	40	207	257	304	528	1,029
Poll tax 1987-88	677	677	677	677	677	677	677
Gain or loss:							
1 adult	-164	-637	-470	-420	-373	-149	352
2 adults	-841	-1,314	-1,147	-1,097	-1,050	-826	-325
3 adults	-1,518	-1,991	-1,824	-1,774	-1,727	-1,503	-1,002
4 adults	-2,195	-2,668	-2,501	-2,451	-2,404	-2,180	-1,679

(Source: CIPFA, *Paying for Local Government, Beyond the Green Paper, Update* (supplement), 1987)

of adults in the household. In general, 'high' spending local authorities with low domestic rates and a high non-domestic rate *lose*, while 'low' spending local authorities with high domestic rates and a low non-domestic rate *gain*.

What does this mean for regions and individual households? Regions in the North and North West with the highest levels of unemployment will pay more, whilst people in the South East and central Midlands will pay less. Inner cities, in particular London, will be particularly heavily hit.

Households with more than two adults are likely to lose, as will people living in properties with a low rateable value. Single adult households and those in high rateable property will gain. However, this will depend on where they live. In areas such as inner London, even single adults and people in higher rateable property will lose from the changes.

References

1 *House of Commons Hansard*, 29 June 1986.
2 John Gibson, *Public Service and Local Government*, June 1987.
3 T Travers, *Times Educational Supplement*, 10 July 1987.
4 House of Commons Paper, 10 July 1987, DoE, 0301/8788(15).
5 C Brown, *Black and White Britain*, Policy Studies Institute, 1984.
6 See *Poll Tax, A Background Information Pack*, Local Government Information Unit, 1987, for more local information.

Chapter 6

Conclusion

It is not by chance that no other country in the Organisation for Economic Co-operation and Development finances local government from a poll tax. The principle that the level of taxation should be adjusted to ability to pay has been accepted as fundamental.

The main focus of this pamphlet is a critique of the poll tax, rather than an analysis of alternative forms of local taxation. It is therefore impossible to do justice to the alternation options for reform such as a local income tax in the space available.[1]

However, there is a strong case for a reformed rating system as the foundation for a local tax. Rates tax that scarce resource — property. They have the advantage of being a predictable source of revenue and are easy to collect. Reforms such as basing domestic and non-domestic rates on capital values would take account of rising property prices, thereby making rates more progressive. The extension of rates to agricultural land would broaden the tax base. Restoring the cuts in housing benefit and improving take-up would be a short-term improvement for people on low incomes. In the long term, there would have to be serious consideration of a uniform system of housing support which amalgamated housing benefit with the so far untouched resources tied up in mortgage interest tax relief.[2]

Meanwhile, what will the poll tax bring?

• It will bring a mass of new officials to collect and maintain a register which has serious implications for civil liberties — personal files will be cross-checked and an identity card system may be required.

• It will provide a direct incentive not to register to vote or use local authority services, as both will provide the basis for collecting names for the poll tax register.

• As a flat-rate tax, entirely unrelated to people's ability to pay, the poll tax will fall most heavily on the poorest sections of society, while at the same time giving a bonanza to the rich.

44

- The poll tax will be highest in many areas where poverty is greatest — inner cities (in particular inner London), and the North and North East, where the unemployment rate has been persistently high.

- Social security claimants, living in areas where the poll tax is above average, will experience real cuts in their income in order to meet the 20% contribution.

- The poll tax will necessitate a hugely complex rebate system, which will extend the poverty trap to a further million people.

- Far from increasing local accountability in the generally understood sense of the words, the poll tax will create a distorted form of accountability. Financial gearing will mean that for every extra pound a local authority spends, an additional £4 falls on the elector. The poorest will bear the brunt of this distorted accountability.

The poll tax is part of a general trend which has characterised the last eight or nine years of government — the centralisation of state control and the promotion of the free market principle, the former enforcing the latter. Hence the double-speak of 'local accountability' and the reality of a tightening rein of central government control over local government's spending power and political voice. The poll tax is also part of an overall economic strategy to reduce public expenditure and a highly regressive tax policy which has shifted the burden from the rich to the poor.

The introduction of the poll tax does have precedents: in the 14th century the feudal government tried to introduce a levy on every adult. Today, the reintroduction of a universal tax entirely unrelated to people's ability to pay has to be condemned. This pamphlet adds one more voice to the growing number opposed to the poll tax, in the hope that the more voices that are heard, the greater the chance they will be heeded.

References
1 See *A Feudal Levy*, CPAG, 1987.
2 See *A New Deal for Home Owners and Tenants*, Association of Metropolitan Authorities, 1987.

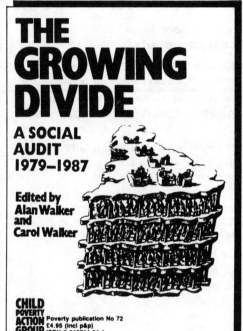

Now's the time to join CPAG!

We can help you . . . with the facts on poverty.
You can help us . . . in the fight against poverty.

CPAG membership gives you access to all the latest – on welfare rights, income inequalities, perspectives on policy, and lots more!

And CPAG members give us the support we need to ensure that poverty is at the heart of the agenda, whatever political party is in power.

Send off the form now, and join CPAG in working for a fairer future.

Please complete and send to: CPAG, 4th Floor, 1-5 Bath Street, London EC1V 9PY.

- -

I would like to join CPAG as a comprehensive member .... (tick)
(Comprehensive members receive CPAG's regular journal, Poverty, plus welfare rights and social policy publications – for £30/year).

or I would like information about other membership options .... (tick)

I enclose a cheque/PO (made out to CPAG) for £30 .... (tick)

Name _____

Organisation (if applicable) _____

Address _____

_____

_____ Postcode _____